U0479890

图书在版编目（CIP）数据

爬行动物 /（英）哥瑞斯·琼斯著；邢敏娟译 . —西安：世界图书出版西安有限公司，2018.1

（我的动物朋友）

ISBN 978-7-5192-3783-7

Ⅰ . ①爬… Ⅱ . ①哥… ②邢… Ⅲ . ①爬行纲—青少年读物 Ⅳ . ① Q959.6-49

中国版本图书馆 CIP 数据核字（2017）第 276387 号

First published in England in 2017 by Booklife Publishing.
Text and illustrations copyright © 2017 Booklife Publishing.
Bilingual: English-Simplified Chinese translation copyright © 2017 by World Publishing Xi'an Co. Ltd.
Bilingual: English-Simplified Chinese audio, video and APP copyright © 2017 by World Publishing Xi'an Co. Ltd.
All rights reserved.
本书仅限中国大陆地区发行销售。

书　　名	爬行动物（我的动物朋友）
著　　者	[英]哥瑞斯·琼斯
译　　者	邢敏娟
策划编辑	陈宇彤
责任编辑	陈宇彤
装帧设计	新纪元文化传播
出版发行	世界图书出版西安有限公司
地　　址	西安市北大街 85 号
邮　　编	710003
电　　话	029-87214941　87233647（市场营销部） 029-87234767（总编室）
网　　址	http://www.wpcxa.com
邮　　箱	xast@wpcxa.com
经　　销	新华书店
印　　刷	鹤山雅图仕印刷有限公司
开　　本	787mm×1092mm　1/12
印　　张	4
字　　数	20 千字
版　　次	2018 年 1 月第 1 版　2018 年 1 月第 1 次印刷
版权登记	25-2017-0061
国际书号	ISBN 978-7-5192-3783-7
定　　价	45.00 元

版权所有　翻印必究
（如有印装错误，请与出版社联系）

我的动物朋友

爬行动物

［英］哥瑞斯·琼斯 / 著

邢敏娟 / 译

动物王国

世界图书出版公司
西安 北京 上海 广州

本书英文原版为英国国家图书馆馆藏图书。本书与英国、美国、加拿大三大英语系国家同步出版。

目录

第 4–5 页

什么是生物？

第 6–7 页

什么是爬行动物？

第 8–9 页

它们的栖息地

第 10–11 页

爬行动物的家园

第 12–13 页

它们的食性

第 14–15 页

它们如何呼吸？

第 16–17 页

它们如何行动？

第 18–19 页

它们如何生长？

第 20–21 页

引人注目的爬行动物

第 22–23 页

打破世界纪录的爬行动物

什么是生物？

所有的生物都具有生长、发育、繁殖的能力。

生物需要空气、营养、水和阳光。

这些都是生物。

青蛙　　老虎　　人类

刀，叉，
盘子。

书

这些都是
非生物。

非生物不具有生长、发育、
繁殖的能力。非生物不需要
空气、营养、水或阳光，因
为它们没有生命气息。

泰迪熊

什么是爬行动物？

爬行动物是可以在水中和陆地上生存的生物。它们的生存离不开空气、食物、水和阳光。蜥蜴、乌龟和鳄鱼，都属于爬行动物。

蜥蜴

乌龟

鳄鱼

爬行动物属于脊椎动物，全身长满**鳞片**，通常在陆地上产卵。它们是冷血动物，它们的体温会随着外界温度的变化而变化。

鳞片

卵

资料：

我们已知的爬行动物有9500多种。

它们的栖息地？

所有的生物都有它们的**栖息地**或家园。一些爬行动物生活在水边或者水中，包括雨林、海洋和河流。

地球上其他一些爬行动物则生活在干燥的陆地、沙漠、山脉和草原。

爬行动物的家园

爬行动物生活在世界上很多不同的地方。对于蛇来说，它们一般生活在地下巢穴。地下巢穴给它们庇护，是它们躲避**捕食者**的避难所，也是它们隐藏蛇卵的安全之地。

毒蛇窝

一些爬行动物生活在 **气候** 炎热的地区，比如沙漠，那里每年只有很少的降雨。这些爬行动物，比如蜥蜴，只需要很少的水就能生活，并且让自己尽量远离太阳的炙热。

沙漠带刺蜥蜴

它们的食性

大部分爬行动物都是**食肉动物**。它们以鸟、老鼠和鱼等小型动物为食。而蛇和鳄鱼的**猎物**会大很多，比如鹿、水牛和斑马。

资料：

一些爬行动物不需要喝水，因为它们会通过皮肤摄取水分。

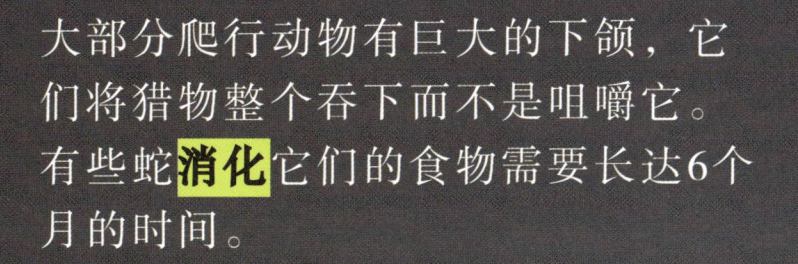

大部分爬行动物有巨大的下颌，它们将猎物整个吞下而不是咀嚼它。有些蛇消化它们的食物需要长达6个月的时间。

一条绿色的毒蛇张开大嘴吞食蜥蜴。

巨大的下颌

它们如何呼吸？

几乎所有的爬行动物都通过它们的两肺进行呼吸。它们通过活动肋骨和胃之间的肌肉来呼吸。

资料：

有些蛇类仅通过一个肺来进行呼吸。

一些乌龟能够在水下呼吸，比如麝香龟，它能用舌头吸收水中的氧气。

麝香龟生活在北美的淡水湖和河流中。

它们如何行动？

大部分爬行动物用它们强壮的腿来爬行。鳄鱼利用它们的尾巴来游泳。一些蜥蜴可以通过断尾来逃脱捕食者的猎杀。

一只断尾的蜥蜴。

爬行动物没有腿，比如蛇，它们利用肋骨和肌肉帮助它们沿地面爬行。它们也会利用鳞片来抓地，从而帮助它们爬行。

蛇骨

肌肉

鳞片

它们如何生长？

大部分爬行动物在**孵化**前，都生活在卵里（卵生动物）。它们通常利用牙齿或身体的力量破壳而出。而有些爬行动物则是胎生动物，比如某些蛇和蜥蜴。

孵化之后，一些爬行动物的父母会继续照顾和喂养下一代，直到它们完全成年。对于某些种类的乌龟来说，这个过程可能短则几周，长则三十多年。

加拉巴哥岛龟

引人注目的
爬行动物

爬行动物色彩艳丽。豹纹变色龙生活在马达加斯加的热带雨林中，它们会在激怒时变成红色或黄色。

一些蜥蜴拥有吓走捕食者的妙招。
澳大利亚伞蜥蜴会张开颈部的伞状皮膜来吓唬其他动物。

打破世界纪录的
爬行动物

咸水鳄

纪录：
世界上最大的爬行动物！

尺寸：
身体长达 6 米

资料：
咸水鳄生活在澳大利亚的河流和小溪中，它们的寿命长达 70 年。

蝙蝠龙（双型齿翼龙）

纪录：
世界上最怪异的爬行动物。

资料：
蝙蝠龙生活在恐龙时代，它们是已知唯一会飞的爬行动物。

尺寸：
身体长达3米

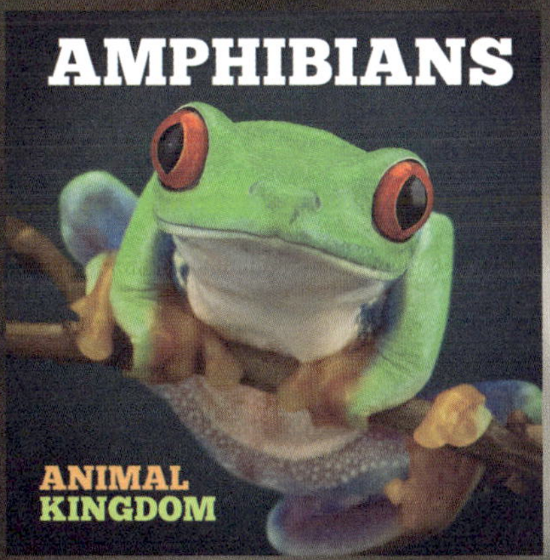

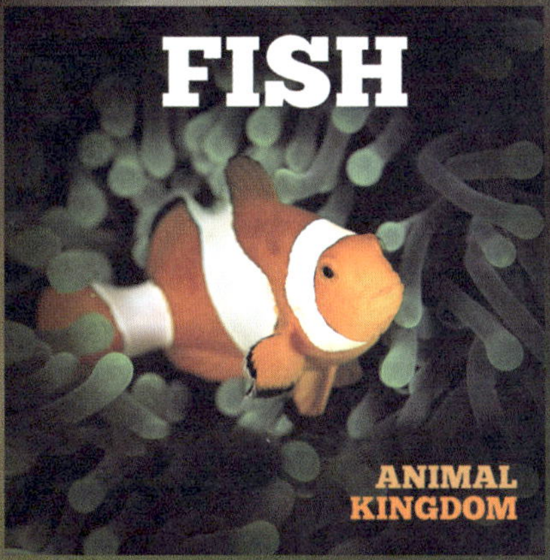

ANIMAL KINGDOM

What is a living thing? Where do animals live? What do animals eat? How do they move and grow?

Learn the answers to these questions in this exciting new series. With easy to read text and informative diagrams, this series offers a simple introduction to the animals that live in our world.

FISH
ANIMAL KINGDOM

REPTILES
ANIMAL KINGDOM

AMPHIBIANS
ANIMAL KINGDOM

BIRDS
ANIMAL KINGDOM

MAMMALS
ANIMAL KINGDOM

INSECTS
ANIMAL KINGDOM

Glossary

carnivores animals that feed on other animals rather than plants

climates types of weather in a particular place

digest to break down food into things that can be used by the body

habitat a home where animals and plants live

hatch when young come out of an egg

predators animals that eat other animals and insects.

prey any animal that is hunted by another

scales small circles of thin bone that protect the skin of fish and reptiles

Index

Air 4 – 6, 14
bodies 7, 16, 18
breathe 14 – 15
chameleons 20
crocodiles 6, 12, 16, 22
eggs 7, 18
food 6, 13
grow 4 – 5, 18 – 19
land 6 – 7, 9
lizards 6, 11, 13, 16, 18, 21
move 14, 16 – 17
scales 7, 17
snakes 10, 12 – 14, 17 – 18
tortoise 6, 19
water 4 – 6, 8, 11 – 12, 15

Photo Credits

Abbreviations: l–left, r–right, b–bottom, t–top, c–centre, m–middle.

Front Cover: TheLightPainter, 1–Kutelvaserova Stuchelova, 2/3–reptiles4all, 4bl–Chros, 4c–Eric Isselee, 4bl–Chros, 4bl–reptiles4all, 4bl–Chros, 4c–Eric Isselee, 4r–michaeljung, 5bl–Elena Schweitzer, 5ll–koosen, 5r–Lichtmeister, 6t–Olga_Serova, 6m–Svetoslav Radkov, 6b–nathanan726, 7–Heiko kiera, 8–Attila JANDI, 9–Janelle Lugge, 10–dmitryGo, 11–Amy Nichole Harris, 12–Kutelvaserova Stuchelova, 13–Trafcus, 14–nathanan726, 15–Marek Velechovsky, 16–Matt Jeppson, 17t–bluehand, 17b–Graphic Compressor, 18–Trevor kelly, 19–ANDRZEJ GRZEGORCZYK, 20–Arto Hakola, 21–Eric Isselee, 22–Volodymyr Burdiak, 23–Catmando. Images are courtesy of Shutterstock.com. With thanks to Getty Images, Thinkstock Photo and iStockphoto.

DIMORPHODON

Record: The World's Weirdest Reptile

Size: Up to 3 metres long

Fact: The only known **flying reptile** to ever exist. Dimorphodon lived when **dinosaurs** were around!

23

World Record Breakers

SALTWATER CROCODILE

Record: The World's Biggest Reptile!

Size: Up to 6 metres long

Fact: Saltwater crocodiles live in the rivers and creeks of Australia and live for up to 70 years.

Some lizards have found clever ways to scare their predators. The Frill-Necked lizard from Australia fans out the skin around its neck to frighten other animals.

Remarkable Reptiles

Reptiles can be very colourful. The Panther chameleon lives in the rainforests of Madagascar and can change colour to red or yellow when it is angry.

After they hatch, some reptile parents continue to look after and feed their young. Their young continue to grow and change until they are fully grown adults. This can take anywhere from a few weeks to more than thirty years for some species of tortoise.

Galapagos Tortoise

How Do They Grow?

Most reptiles start life inside their mother's eggs before they are ready to **hatch**. They usually cut through their eggshells with their teeth or break them using their bodies. Other reptiles, including some snakes and lizards, give birth to live young.

Reptiles without legs, such as snakes, use bones called ribs and muscles to help to move themselves along the ground. They also use their scales to help them to grip the ground as they are moving.

Snake Bones

Muscles

Scales

17

How Do They Move?

Most reptiles use their strong legs to help them to move their bodies. Crocodiles use their tails to help them swim, while some lizards can shed their tails to help them run away from predators.

A lizard who has shed its tail.

Some species of turtle are able to breathe underwater. The Common Musk turtle is able to take in air underwater because it can absorb oxygen in the water through its tongue.

The Common Musk turtle is found in the freshwater lakes and rivers of North America.

How Do They Breathe?

Almost all reptiles breathe oxygen from the air through their two lungs. Reptiles move the muscles in-between their ribs and stomach to breathe in and out.

Fact: Some snake species breathe through only one lung.

Most reptiles have large jaws and swallow their prey whole rather than chewing it. It can take as long as six months for some snakes to **digest** their food!

A Venom Green snake opens its jaws to eat a lizard.

Large Jaws

What Do They Eat?

Almost all reptiles are **carnivores**. They eat small animals, such as birds, mice and fish. Snakes and crocodiles are known to eat much larger **prey**, such as deer, buffalo and zebra.

Fact:
Some reptiles don't need to drink any water because they absorb it through their skin.

Some reptiles live in very hot **climates**, such as desert habitats, which get very little rain every year. Reptiles, such as lizards, can live on little water and try to keep themselves out of the sun's heat as much as possible.

Desert Spiny Lizard

Reptile Homes

Reptiles can live in many different habitats found around the world. A common habitat for snakes is under the ground in a cave or a nest. Their underground homes provide them with shelter from **predators** and a safe place to hide their eggs.

Viper Nest

6

Other reptiles live on dry land, in the deserts, mountains and grasslands found on planet Earth.

Where Do They Live?

All living things live in a **habitat** or home. Some reptiles live near to or in water, including in rainforests, oceans and rivers.

Reptiles have **scales** all over their bodies, have backbones and usually lay their eggs on land. They are also cold-blooded animals. This means that their body temperature changes when the temperature outside gets hotter or colder.

Fact: **There are over 9,500 known species of reptile.**

Scales

Eggs

What Is a Reptile?

Rteptiles are living things that can live in water and on land. They need air, food, water and sunlight to live. Lizards, tortoises and crocodiles are all types of reptile.

Lizard

Tortoise

Crocodile

Knife, fork & plate.

Books

These are all non-living things.

Non-living things do not have the ability to grow, develop and reproduce. Non-living things do not need air, nutrition, water or sunlight because they are not alive.

Teddy Bear

What Are Living Things?

All living things have the ability to grow, develop and reproduce. Living things need air, nutrition, water and sunlight to stay alive.

These are all living things.

Frog

Tiger

Human

4

Contents

Pages 4-5
What Are Living Things?

Pages 6-7
What is a Reptile?

Pages 8-9
Where Do They Live?

Pages 10-11
Reptile Homes

Pages 12-13
What Do They Eat?

Pages 14-15
How Do They Breathe?

Pages 16-17
How Do They Move?

Pages 18-19
How Do They Grow?

Pages 20-21
Remarkable Reptiles

Pages 22-23
World Record Breakers

Page 24
Glossary & Index

A catalogue record for this book is available from the British Library.

Words that appear like **this** can be found in the glossary on page 24.

ANIMAL KINGDOM

REPTILES

Grace Jones

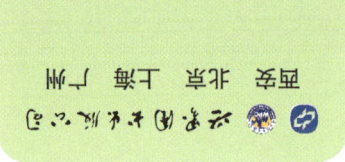